YOUR WORDS HAVE POWER!

Learning the Art of Healthy Communication

Shawn Adams

Editorial Midwife Publishing

Ordering Information
For quantity sales, special discounts may be available for corporations, associations, and others. Contact the author at adamsshawn89@gmail.com.

Editor & Consultant
Lita P. Ward, The Editorial Midwife
LPW Editing & Consulting Services, LLC
Editorial Midwife Publishing
www.litapward.com / lpwediting@gmail.com

Cover Design
BVS Consulting, LLC
bvsconsultingltd@gmail.com

ISBN: 9798859300334

Printed in USA

Dedication

To my husband and best friend, Mark Adams:

I'm grateful to God for all of your support and guidance. You encourage me to be excellent in every aspect of my life. Life is amazing because I share it with an amazing Man of God.

CONTENTS

INTRODUCTION

In my 15 years of pastoring people, I have discovered people generally have difficulty conveying their thoughts and feelings verbally. The more I spoke to people, the more I heard the same problem. As I reminisce over my own life, I realize there were times I didn't utilize healthy communication. I wanted to help people, and I wanted to help myself in the process. Often, when God gives you a word to help others, the word is meant to help you first. Healthy communication was something my husband and I had to work hard at. It wasn't fixed overnight. There were days we had victory and times we felt defeated in our communication. God began to speak to me about strategies on how to help people become better communicators. Out of those strategies, this book was written. I want to encourage every reader to share the content with family and friends. I believe we have the ability to impart healthy communication to everyone we meet.

Please take the opportunity to jot down notes or your thoughts in the sections provided. Take your time and receive the full benefits from the information and insight provided. This should be a journey, not a race.

CHAPTER 1

Healthy Communication

Communication has defects, but I believe it can become healthy communication when given the correct tools. If you don't fix the deficiencies in your communication, your relationship may not stand the test of time. Healthy communication is articulating your thoughts and feelings to another person. Healthy communication must be accompanied by what is factual and less by what is driven by your emotions.

Your communication style is not for you! Your communication style is for the person you are communicating with. Often, people say, "This is just how I am" or "This is how I speak." Just because you have communicated the same way all your life does not make it right. These statements validate the fact that there are some errors in your communication. Still, you must be willing to make the necessary changes.

In most cases, you adopted a communication style from the environment you grew up in. Sometimes, the communication style is unhealthy, but it is a learned behavior. We must break the curse of unhealthy communication. As parents, you teach your children to communicate by the way we communicate with them. Parents should not be surprised when their child imitates their communication style. Therefore, the cycle of unhealthy communication must be broken! Parents who use unhealthy communication should not be upset when their child sounds like them! Nor surprised when their child mimics words they have heard at home.

So, let's get to work. The following principles and scriptural references will steer your journey to healthy communication within your home and among your relationships.

Principle 1: *Strive to Live in Peace and Unity*

Conflict from unhealthy communication is common in families not equipped to communicate. Ephesians 4:1-3 (NIV) states, "As a prisoner for the Lord, then, I urge you to live a life worthy of the calling you have received. Be completely humble and gentle; be patient, bearing with one another in love. Make every effort to keep the unity of the Spirit through the bond of peace."

A popular phrase is "I'm protecting my peace." This phrase exemplifies that a person has decided to control their environment and control who disrupts it. You are not protecting your peace when you allow people to dictate your day by how they feel. When people know that they can alter your day by their words, they understand they have control over you. Protecting your peace is controlling your day. This could mean separating yourselves from family members you talk to daily.

What if the person who disrupted your day was your own mother? How would you handle this? How would you separate from the person who gave you life? *"Do not think that I have come to bring peace to the earth; I have not come to bring peace, but a sword. For I have come to set a man against his father, and a daughter against her mother, and a daughter-in-law against her mother-in-law; and one's foes will be members of one's own household"* (Matthew 10:34-36). There will be times in your life when your own family will appear to be your worst enemy.

In addition, Jesus states that we must understand that personal things will arise and try to get us to move from following Him. Then Jesus said to his disciples, "Whoever wants to be my disciple must deny themselves and take up their cross and follow me (Matthew 16:24, NIV). We must be willing to deny everything and everyone to take up our cross and follow Jesus, even if it's a family member.

I have counseled many people who had to disconnect from a family member for a season. During this season, God will sometimes deal with the person you are disconnecting from if they have a willing spirit to receive His direction and correction. The person disconnecting should always communicate the reason for the disconnect. This allows the person an opportunity to correct their behavior.

Psalms 133 :1 (NIV) states, "How good and pleasant it is when God's people live together in unity." However, sometimes you may need to temporarily separate from someone to find peace and unity. The good news is the season of separation doesn't last forever but only until a healthy way of communicating develops.

To fix the broken places of communication, you must know your triggers. The enemy uses triggers to get you to act out of character. A trigger is an action or situation that can lead to an adverse emotional reaction. Your spouse or family member experiencing a bad day at work can be a trigger. Your children having a rough day at school can be a trigger. The enemy will use people close to you to disrupt your day. He chooses people close to you because he knows this is a place of weakness for most people. When a person is triggered, they have uncomfortable emotions that cause a negative response. A triggered person may feel overwhelmed with anger, cry, act out of character, or react defensively. Although triggers are different for everyone, trigger symptoms are often the same. *Do you know your triggers? If so, list them below:*

_____

_____

_____

_____

_____

_____

_____

_____

_____

_____

_____

_____

Principle 2: *Know the Tactics of Satan*

The one thing I have discovered about Satan is he duplicates what he believes is working. You must be willing to do something different to defeat Satan at his tactics. Satan has identified your patterns. He has identified the things that get you off your game. He has identified the things that are hidden from others but are revealed to him.

The tactic of Satan is to use what is familiar and keep using it until it BREAKS you. Have you ever noticed that month after month and year after year, you experience the same trial? The trials are repeating themselves because Satan has discovered the very thing that gets you every time. Satan doesn't have to think or try to create something new for you when what he has been using works so well. What can you identify from this principle as satanic tactics used in your life?

_____

_____

_____

_____

_____

_____

_____

Principle 3: *Know Your Triggers*

You have to know yourself! You must do some soul-searching to discover what triggers your behavior and causes you to live a life that contradicts Jesus Christ. As previously stated, Satan has studied you and identified your weaknesses, but sadly, we don't know our weaknesses. For the most part, we like to appear as though we have everything together and don't have areas of weakness. Most certainly, this is furthest from the truth! Self-examination is the study of one's own behavior and motivations. It removes finger-pointing and places the focus back on you.

Here is an example of how the enemy will use your marriage as a trigger: A couple was recently married, and things tend to go well during the honeymoon stages. The honeymoon stage is when the union is still fresh. There have not been any disagreements yet. Everything is good until one day, an argument erupts over something small. Now the enemy can blow the situation up and make it appear worse than it is. This argument has now triggered a place of doubt. Now one of them is thinking they married the wrong person. There are thoughts of divorce, leaving, and never returning. The minor disagreement has triggered other emotions causing them to speak unwholesome words to the person they love. This is the entryway for the enemy to come in and steal from the unaware couple.

The enemy steals the joy, peace, love, and intimacy from your marriage! Too often, we do not recognize that he uses what is near and dear to our hearts. Ephesians 4:29 (NIV) says, " Do not let unwholesome talk come out of your mouths, but only what helps build others up according to their needs, that it may benefit those who listen." Identify your triggers and list them. Vulnerability and transparency are critical!

_____

_____

_____

_____

_____

_____

_____

_____

_____

_____

_____

_____

Let's look closer into self-examination to ensure you have clarity for proper application and execution. Once the self-examination is complete, you are ready to work on your communication!

In my opinion, the proper way to examine yourself is to examine yourself through the eyes of God. Self-examination requires you to have a personal relationship with God so that you may hear His voice and understand His Word. Then ask yourself what God's Word says about self-examination.

"Search me, God, and know my heart; test me and know my anxious thoughts. See if there is any offensive way in me and lead me in the way everlasting" (Psalms 139: 23-24, NIV). This Scripture gives us the winning equation for godly self-examination in three steps:

1. Search my heart and thoughts.
2. Remove any offensive ways in me to God and man.
3. Lead me in the way that I may please God forever.

Describe how you can apply this Scripture to your own self-examination. Take this opportunity to be transparent and honest with God and yourself.

_____

_____

CHAPTER 2

Identifying Your Communication Style

Your communication style is broken down into four styles. Which style best describes how you communicate?

1. Passive Communicator

The word "passive" can be perceived as soft or a pushover. The definition of passive is accepting or allowing what happens or what others do without active response or resistance. A Passive Communicator cannot express what is happening in their mind, leading to misunderstanding, resentment, and anger. A passive communicator thinks the other party should know their thoughts or feelings. They have a difficult time verbally expressing their feelings. Passive Communicators feel their feelings are overlooked but don't share them. They are passive in their communication style. On the flip side, a Passive Communicator is good at de-escalating situations. They are less likely to be confrontational and aggressive.

Passive Communicators usually lack eye contact, and they have poor body language. They also cannot say no.

They generally want everyone to be happy, and they are people pleasers. Instead of confronting them, they let things pass on by. For example, their response will be, *"It doesn't matter,"* or *"I just want to keep the peace."* Passive Communicators are so focused on keeping the peace that they are willing to disregard their thoughts and opinions.

2. Aggressive Communicator

The word "aggressive" has a negative connotation. Aggressive means ready or likely to attack or confront. I call these types of communicators the Angry Birds! They are usually loud communicators and have deeper issues that must be addressed. If a communicator is hollering and screaming, there is a BIGGER ISSUE called anger that must be dealt with. They are very demanding and use the art of intimidation to get their partner to back down. They love to make threats and throw objects while communicating.

In most cases, warning signs are present. Still, we love the Aggressive Communicator so much we miss the warning before the destruction. They will command rather than ask. People are inwardly afraid of an aggressive communicator. Here is an example of their communication: *"I'm really starting to get irritated with this conversation! Hurry up and say what you really mean. I'm so over this!"*

An Aggressive Communicator goes from zero to 100 in a matter of minutes. They usually battle with this spirit of anger, but they have not identified the root cause of their anger in most cases.

3. Passive-Aggressive Communicator

A Passive-Aggressor Communicator is what I call a combo communicator. They are a combination of passive and aggressive all in one person. This person appears to be passive on the surface but feels they are overlooked. When they finally speak up, it comes out aggressively because they have built up resentment from not expressing themselves. When resentful, people sometimes start making secret moves out of their emotions. They are like a pipe waiting to burst because of all the pressure.

Another sign of the Passive-Aggressor Communicator is they mummer and complain to themselves instead of addressing the issue. They have a difficult time expressing themselves. Denying there is a problem, the Passive-Aggressor Communicator usually communicates with their body language. They act like they are cooperating, but silently, they are against you. Your example of communication for this style is, *"Sure, I don't mind helping.*

But I'm so sick of helping people. No one was there for me when I needed help."

4. Assertive Communicator

An Assertive Communicator is a communicator we should all strive to be more like. This communicator is unlike any of the others we previously discussed. This is the most effective style of communication. This is the person concerned about themselves and the person they are communicating with. They can express their needs and feelings, but they also want to hear about the needs and feelings of the other person. This is a win-win for everyone! Here are two prime examples of their positive communication: *"I will let you speak first, and after you're done, I will better understand how the miscommunication happened"* or *"Let me apologize for my part in the miscommunication."*

Now that we have recognized the four communication styles, which resonates with you more than the others? Explain why. What can you do to become a more positive communicator?

_____

_____

_____

In this space, take the time to recall what you have learned thus far about how you communicate with others. Recall how others have responded back to you during difficult conversations. What do you plan to do differently or implement to promote healthier conversations?

_____

_____

_____

_____

_____

_____

_____

_____

_____

_____

_____

_____

_____

_____

_____

_____

_____

_____

CHAPTER 3

The Absence of Agreement in Communication

"It Takes Two"

Again, truly I tell you that if two of you on earth agree about anything they ask for, it will be done for them by my Father in heaven (Matthew 18:19, NIV)

It has been said, "Two heads are better than one." Therefore, the power of agreement is most effective when healthy communication is present. In a nutshell, agreement is getting two or more people on the same page in any context. Agreement is also being likeminded, having the same love, and being one in spirit. It is not a one-person show or a sole performance when agreement exists. The mission now becomes how we can get this done together.

Oftentimes, you will have to find a place to compromise. It's not about getting your way but *finding* a way to work with your partner. The agreement is a two-person job! You're much stronger when working together towards a common goal. Don't get comfortable working alone. Have you ever had a dream on hold because you didn't have anyone to share it with? Contrary to popular belief, we need people who help cheer us on to complete goals, which also gives us the element of accountability. It takes two to make a thing go right, so don't fear collaboration.

On the flip side, some agreements are toxic. Listed are a few examples of toxic agreements:

- Being in a relationship with a physical, verbal, or emotional abuser
- Being in a relationship with a person who has narcissistic behaviors.
- Being in a relationship with a person who has trust issues.

Here is an example of how effectively you can use the power of agreement:

My husband and I were contemplating adding a bonus room to our home. We had enough land that adding the room would not detract from our backyard. The problem became the costs due to the rising cost of lumber. After an evaluation and speaking to a few contractors, it was determined that adding a bonus room could cost up to $50,000! This was more than we were expecting. If the cost of lumber had been lower, the same bonus room would have cost us $12,000. My husband and I agreed that now was not the time, so we added a covered deck instead. This option was a win for both of us. We were still able to create additional space for entertaining the family. We were also able to add a flat-screen television to make the space even more enjoyable! We could have delayed the project until the lumber prices went down, but we found a way to compromise. Agreement is more about communicating and compromising.

You will miss the beauty of agreement if you cannot share your innermost thoughts. I encourage you to open up and begin to share. Sharing your dreams, visions, ideas, and goals with the right person can be a game-changer for your future. You must also be willing to be vulnerable with areas of your life that you have hidden. God wants to heal what you have concealed. It isn't easy to heal from the areas you have covered up for so long, but healing is available to you.

We live in a day and time where people have mastered operating broken. We have learned to bury the pain because judgment is attached to what we deal with daily. There are so many open wounds that have not properly healed. There are wounds from relationships and your childhood. There are wounds from losing a loved one, abandonment, and rejection. Because the wounds have not properly healed, we continue to live broken. The absence of agreement will cause you to harbor feelings of your hurt, which can eventually lead to a bigger problem. It's time to release all the frustration the absence of agreement brings to your life.

Let's utilize this space to uncover any open wounds that need healing or dreams you have placed on hold. In addition, identify areas you can incorporate the power of agreement.

_____

_____

_____

_____

_____

_____

_____

_____

_____

_____

CHAPTER 4

How to Handle a Misunderstanding

A misunderstanding generally stems from a communication breakdown. You may have heard it one way, but that was not the intention of the person delivering the message. Becoming a better communicator makes you less likely to offend people.

Hearing that you hurt someone with your words is not easy to digest. We usually don't want to hurt the person we love. However, some people have a difficult time taking ownership of their words. It can be tough to hear, "You hurt me when you said..." The recipient of the message would rather be praised than criticized. Depending on the person's open-mindedness, the conversation could go well or escalate quickly. Hating to hear that you hurt someone and not being able to apologize is a flaming combination.

In most cases, an apology is given when a person has wronged someone they love. Reconciliation comes quicker when there is a sincere apology. In life, you will not always get an apology. Sometimes, you just have to move on without it.

In Matthew 12:36, the disciple Matthew instructs us to choose our words wisely to reduce misunderstandings. "But I tell you that everyone will have to give an account on the day of judgment for every empty word they have spoken."

An empty word is defined as talking with little meaning. This is when the message you convey seems to have substance but does not. Let's dive deeper into the effects of empty words.

- **Failure to Understand:** Jesus replied, "You are in error because you do not know the Scriptures or the power of God" (Matthew 22:29). A misunderstanding can arise when you do not understand. Clearing up a misunderstanding due to a failure to understand is like hitting the reset button. Sometimes, you just have to start over and change your verbiage so the listener can gain understanding. Patience is key! Be willing to stop and focus on finding a resolution that works for everyone involved.

- **Failure to Properly Articulate:** Broken communication is from broken articulation! You didn't explain it well if you omitted vital facts that needed to be stated. I'm a visual person. As a person speaks to me, I'm forming a picture in my mind. Sometimes my visions are spot on, and sometimes they miss the mark. When I formulate the correct vision, it's usually because the person gave so many details. The lack of content gives birth to a distorted vision. So, say what you mean!

- **Assumptions:** Stop thinking you know what a person is thinking before they say it! Be patient enough to wait for them to articulate their thoughts. Contrary to popular belief, you don't know everything. Assumptions can damage your ability to relate to others. You will stop listening and communicating if you think you know what a person feels or is thinking. Undoubtedly, that will lead to a misunderstanding.

- **Lack of Content:** Have you ever spoken to someone whose message lacked content? Misunderstandings form when your complaints or concerns have no depth or meaning. There's no other way to explain the lack of content other than just saying, "I don't get it." Sometimes you have to agree to disagree when it comes to a misunderstanding.

Typically, how do you handle misunderstandings? Did you find yourself in any of the *empty words* concepts? If yes, how do you propose to change your message when communicating with others?

_____

_____

_____

_____

_____

_____

_____

_____

_____

_____

_____

_____

_____

_____

_____

_____

_____

CHAPTER 5

"It's A Man Thing"

This portion of the book is designed to help you understand how a man thinks. I'm thankful I have been able to learn more about how a man thinks through my husband. At no given time am I giving myself credit for knowing the thought process of a man, but I would like to share my knowledge. The one thing I can truly stand on is men and women have different languages. Sometimes the way a man says it is different from what the woman heard. Let's explore a few areas to help you better communicate with a man.

Men vs. Women

Timing: Essentially, proper communication is embedded in the art of knowing the proper timing. Usually, a man wants to take time and process the situation. When a man is processing the situation, he is not as vocal as the woman would like him to be. In his mind, he is replaying what happened, what should have happened, and the next steps going forward. In most cases, he doesn't move abruptly. He is managing his emotions by waiting for the proper discussion time.

On the other hand, the man could possibly not want to talk about it at all and avoids having a conversation. Women, however, don't really take into consideration the proper timing. We want to discuss the situation as soon as it happens. Often, we don't allow ourselves time to get our emotions in check and settle down before wanting to have a conversation. Our emotions can lead us to say things we did not mean. They can also cause you to separate or disconnect from what you need to stay connected to.

Personally, I can think of times when my timing was off. I believe that a couple should not go to bed angry. My timing even caused me to miss sleep because I wanted to deal with the situation immediately. According to Ephesians 4:26-27, "In your anger do not sin. Do not let the sun go down while you are still angry, and do not give the devil a foothold." I grabbed hold of this Scripture but did not use its wisdom in some situations. Wisdom is the quality of having experiences, knowledge, and sound judgment; it must be present to operate at the right time.

Emotions: In my 15 years of pastoring people, I can safely say, "I have encountered men who have made decisions based on their emotions." Society sometimes characterizes a woman as an emotional being. While the expressive component of emotions has been widely studied, it is still unclear whether men or women differ in aspects of emotions. Women are more emotionally expressive. Women utilize their bodies, eyes, and hands as an outward demonstration of their emotions. Positive emotions, like happiness, and negative emotions, like anger, can get in the way of healthy communication.

In healthy communication, you must have emotional awareness. Emotional awareness is the ability to understand feelings. If you are emotionally aware, you will communicate better. Being emotionally aware helps you notice the emotions of yourself and other people. Sometimes, the emotions of others influence the way we communicate. Understanding how a person communicates is sometimes more important than understanding what is being said.

Men and women hide their feelings at some point. Although, hiding your emotions is hard to do for most people. This is because your emotions tell the truth about what you are feeling. You can improve your emotional awareness by focusing on the following things:

1. Take into consideration the other person's feelings.
2. Take into consideration your own feelings.
3. Identify the misunderstanding.
4. Know the heart of the person you are communicating with.
5. Rebuild trust.
6. Have an open mind to receive.

Fact or Feelings: Men tend to have a "report" communication style. Their verbal report contains facts, data, and aims to solve the problem. They tend to leave out personal information about their feelings and how a situation truly affected them. If the woman is not careful, the man will dominate the conversation. A woman, however, uses a "rapport" communication style to build the relationship. This style of communication is built on how the situation made her feel. Facts are rarely presented or sometimes discounted. For women, they understand saying, "I apologize," can resolve many issues.

Conversely, men can see an apology as the other person's way of accepting their authority. Men respond to conversations that get directly to the point. They are thinking, "What is the fact of the matter?" and "How long will it take you to get your point out?" They are ready to move to the next thing, like watching television. Women are diverse. They want to dig until they get to the root of the matter. They are in search of "why." Even though, in some cases, women are emotionally driven, they want to resolve the issue and keep it from happening again.

After learning these concepts, do you better understand how our men communicate? What will you do differently or implement when communicating with them? Once you try these techniques, document the outcomes or responses you received here.

_____

_____

_____

_____

_____

_____

_____

_____

CHAPTER 6

How Do You Fix Unhealthy Communication?

People will devote much time discussing the problem, but how do you fix what is broken? I'm glad you asked! The purpose of this book is to bring resolution to our unhealthy communication. Below, you will find the seven steps to fixing unhealthy communication:

1. Be attentive. Listen without interrupting.
2. Force yourself to hear and not listen to respond.
3. Be open and honest.
4. Address the now.
5. Make a commitment not to repeat the same behavior.
6. Be mindful of your tone and body language.
7. Choose positive words in a negative situation.

1. Be Attentive. Listen Without Interrupting.

Attempting to communicate with interruptions can be difficult. The listener may want to interject a thought. Still, that interjection at the wrong time can be perceived as rude or insensitive. In the listener's mind, they are trying to have a two-way conversation but can't get a word in.

My husband describes this as talking without breathing. Personally, I feel like I'm completing a thought. However, the listener could lose their train of thought due to being unable to interject.

2. Force Yourself to Hear and Not Listen to Respond.

Forcing yourself to hear and not listen to respond takes practice. I believe we all can appreciate the fact that we are connected to people who are good listeners. The speaker can ignite a thought-provoking dialogue. The listener can be so intrigued by the dialogue it causes them to immediately respond. We must also listen with the intent to understand. This is the place where we gain clarity. This is also where you visualize and process what you're hearing in your mind.

3. Be Open and Honest.

Being open and honest puts you in a vulnerable place you don't want to be in. It has advantages and disadvantages when you're genuinely open and honest. An advantage to being open and honest is the listener gains an inside view of your heart. Sometimes, when your heart is exposed, it can be trampled on because the person listening took advantage of what they heard, which is a disadvantage to the speaker. Proverbs 19:1 says, "Better is a poor person who walks in his integrity than one who is crooked in speech and is a fool" (ESV), which means we honor God with our lips by being honest.

King Solomon teaches in Proverbs 6: 16-20 the seven acts that God hates: *There are six things that the Lord hates; seven that are an abomination to him: haughty eyes, a lying tongue, and hands that shed innocent blood, a heart that devises wicked plans, feet that make haste to run to evil, a false witness who breathed out lies, and one who sows discord among brothers. My son, keep your father's commandment and forsake not your mother's teaching.* Lying is an abomination to God! We are quick to find fault in others and highlight their sins, but we miss the fact that, as Christians, we tell lies. God is not pleased with this behavior.

33

4. *Address the Now.*

Addressing the now is having communication that only deals with the current event. When a misunderstanding happens, you may bring up unrelated and unresolved issues. Addressing old issues while having a current event is evidence of unfinished business. As much as possible, live in the now unless the old situation is connected to the current event.

5. *Make a Commitment Not to Repeat the Behavior.*

Nothing is more frustrating than communicating your thoughts and feelings only to discover that the person is still committing the same violations. When your partner shares their innermost feelings, a changed behavior proves they heard them. Sometimes, people will change for a moment but are unwilling to commit to a lifetime of change. Changing in a relationship is for you and the person you are with. Although change can be uncomfortable and difficult, change is necessary when the communication style is toxic.

6. *Be Mindful of Your Tone and Body Language.*

When you are upset, your voice can naturally elevate. Your tone of voice is how you speak to someone, not just your words. We have non-verbal cues that are sometimes more powerful than actual words. Keeping the same tone while communicating in a problematic situation can be the difference between de-escalation and escalating the problem. Our body language has a way of expressing what we are thinking. Try going to a romantic restaurant for a difficult conversation to keep your tone in check. The atmosphere alone can be calming, significantly if the lighting is dimmed and there's jazz music in the background. Try it; I know it works!

As much as possible, remain in the same posture while communicating. Shifting your body can send a non-verbal message that you are ready for the conversation to end. Presentation is essential while communicating. Stay alert so that you may have a clear understanding and positive results.

7. *Choose Positive Words in a Negative Situation.*

Using positive words in negative situations is something that I learned while working in Corporate America. As a Customer Service Manager responsible for de-escalating calls, I used positive words to communicate with the customer. I started the resolution part of the call by telling the customer what I could do for them. When you start your sentence with "unfortunately," the customer expects bad news. Communication with a husband or a friend operates the same way.

Your word choice can create a positive interaction when you understand the meaning of each word. Since words have power, positive words can turn a situation around. I have listed a few examples to help you on your journey to healthy communication:

- X **Negative Communication:** "You never make time for me."

- ✓ **Rephrase:** "Hunny/Bae, I want us to go out more. Do you already have plans for Friday?"

- X **Negative Communication:** "You never support my dreams."
- ✓ **Rephrase:** "I would love for you to be present at my awards ceremony."

- X **Negative Communication:** "You will mess up the clothes if you don't separate them properly."

- ✓ **Rephrase:** "Can you recheck the clothes in the washer?"

In closing, I would like to encourage you that you can change your communication style. You must be willing to adjust and follow the instructions outlined in each chapter. Once you do, you are on your way to healthier communication.

STAY IN CONTACT WITH
APOSTLE SHAWN ADAMS:

Email Address:
adamsshawn89@gmail.com

Facebook Account: Remnant Ministries International | Augusta GA |

NOTES

NOTES

Made in the USA
Middletown, DE
03 September 2024